# FINISHING TOUCHES

### also by Ricardo Quinones

*North/South: The Great European Divide*
(U Toronto P 2016)

*Fringes*
(39 West Press 2015)

*A Sorting of the Ways: New and Selected Poems*
(39 West Press 2011)

*Roberta and Other Poems*
(39 West Press 2011)

*Through the Years*
(39 West Press 2010)

*Erasmus and Voltaire: Why They Still Matter*
(U Toronto P 2010)

*Dualisms: The Agons of the Modern World*
(U Toronto P 2007)

*Foundation Sacrifice in Dante's "Commedia"*
(Penn State UP 1994)

*The Changes of Cain: Violence and the Lost Brother*
(Princeton UP 1991)

*Mapping Literary Modernism: Time and Development*
(Princeton UP 1985)

*Dante Alighieri*
(Twayne 1979; updated revised edition 1998)

*The Renaissance Discovery of Time*
(Harvard UP 1972)

# Finishing Touches

POEMS BY
## Ricardo Quinones

**39 WEST PRESS**

**39 WEST PRESS**
Kansas City, MO
www.39WestPress.com

Copyright © 2014 by Ricardo Quinones

All rights reserved. No part of this book may be reproduced, scanned, or distributed in any printed or electronic form, including information storage and retrieval systems, without permission. Please do not participate in or encourage piracy of copyrighted materials in violation of the author's rights. Please purchase only authorized editions.

First Edition: October 2014

ISBN: 978-0-9908649-0-5

Library of Congress Control Number: 2014952288

This book is a work of fiction. Names, characters, places, dates, and incidents are products of the author's imagination, or are used fictitiously, satirically, or as parody. Any resemblance to actual persons, living or dead, business establishments, events, or locales is entirely coincidental.

10 9 8 7 6 5 4 3 2

*Design, Layout: j.d.tulloch*

*The art-photograph on the back cover
is the work of the very talented Michele Mattei*

39WP-07A

# CONTENTS

*Preface*      i

Incipit      iii

### PART ONE
## Teeming Americana

| | |
|---|---|
| *Author's Note* | 3 |
| SoCal: A Sorting of the Ways | 5 |
| Too Soon Gone | 8 |
| Early and Late: The Hazards of the Ways | 11 |
| Shanksville | 14 |

**Abusives (1-5)**
| | |
|---|---|
|    1. Trucker | 21 |
|    2. The Teacher's Sub | 22 |
|    3. Tante Circe | 24 |
|    4. Marlene | 25 |
|    5. Birds of a Different Feather | 26 |

| | |
|---|---|
| Sudden Glory | 29 |
| Oswego | 31 |
| The Turn of the Stare | 33 |

## PART TWO
## New Poems

| | |
|---|---|
| The Crow | 37 |
| 19 Men | 40 |
| Broken Lilacs | 43 |

**Station Crossings (1-9)**

| | |
|---|---|
| 1. Harry | 45 |
| 2. The End of Tragedy | 47 |
| 3. Cruel Sufferer | 50 |
| 4. Charity and Carnality | 54 |
| 5. Her Books are in Order, Her Mind Intact | 56 |
| 6. This is my mother (of whom I am very proud) | 59 |
| 7. Profusions of Song | 63 |
| 8. Letters to the Home Place | 67 |
| 9. "The wisdom of the wise …" | 70 |
| Laggard | 75 |

# PREFACE

*Finishing Touches* is a purposeful combination of the old and the new. The old is represented by *Teeming Americana* and, as its own preface indicates, opens itself to dramatization. It has its logic in history while the new, *Station Crossings*, tends more towards philosophical gatherings and the quests and the needs of character types. The line of difference is marked by the first of the new poems, "The Crow" and "19 Men," where reality of events seems to contradict the mythography of poetry. "The Coda," in prose, is followed by a "defense of poésie," which then plays its part throughout the new poems. Thus, *Station Crossings* is made up of sections with two poems: the smaller, secondary one intended to counter, augment or disdain the primary, larger venture.

— Ricardo Quinones

# INCIPIT

There they were strung out in a line
Five possum pups trailing their mother's tail
White bellies turned up to the sky
Unable to differ female from male
They followed their mother's imprint
Through a rip in the backyard fence
Along the path that led to the pool
Marched along to their watery grave
Through strangled gulps
They struggled to stay afloat
Too dark and dangerous
What was pulling them down.
Did some such plaint or plea
Of the peril to which they had been brought
Traveling through the sensory system
Finally reach rudimentary thought,
"Why are you doing this to me?"

# PART ONE
# Teeming Americana

# AUTHOR'S NOTE

On November 21, 2013, the four poems that follow were read dramatically by two "redactors," Todd Mandell and Richard Sogliuzzo. My theory was that while poetic drama had fallen into disuse this did not mean that there was not drama in verse. In fact, better than a single person reading, such dramatization brought out the multiple voices within poetry and increased comprehensibility and appeal.

— Ricardo Quinones

## SoCal: A Sorting of the Ways

"All people are the same,"
Breezing she goes over her bubbly,
"Oh no they're not,"
Passing on the fly I let out,
With which I am glad to say
Even my masseuse agreed
She even doubled down on diversity

Thus began my recent run
Of California skirmish
My adopted native land
Once again my chest hollow sinks
At the latest gush of fabled wealth
Flotillas of pricey models
Preen as they parade
Through every street and strip
Barracuda-eyed and snub-nosed
Contoured additions to the terrain

Down that sink-hole cycle
I did not need the vocal brand
"STK PRFT"
On a Bimmer tooling by
"I am glad you spent it dear," I think
"But need you advertise the haul?
Wasn't older wealth more discreet?
They didn't shower in the street."
Democratic ease and sufficient opulence
Was how Whitman wanted it
And particularly better
If the getter knew how it was gotten
Or was somewhat philanthropic.

My heart jumped
When barely an hour later
An apparition rounded the verge
Of my condo complex road
A retired couple—no down-and-outers they—
She quite pert in her synthetic whites
And he slim trim and neatly tucked
Carrying a pick-spade in one
And in the other hand a veggie bag
Something had clearly turned round
The tunings of southern Orange County.

You can bet my converse was eager
Magi never met an equal joy
A communal garden they were tending
And he rattled off the shades of lettuce
Iceberg, romaine, escarole and more
Like Bottom I was delirious
With sweet peas and snap peas
Keep ringing them up, please, I implored
20 x 20 plots of land-fill
With water twenty dollars a year,
I thought we were back with FDR
Pilfering was of no account
They had a renewable resource
And didn't need what they didn't have.

Such sorting of the ways:
Diagonal from these municipal plots
Students zoom up in sporty cars
And uncontrollable apparel
Parents wait their wagons throbbing
Yet symphonists still master on
With brows of concentrated fervor.

My own way stepped far back then
To our own "Victory" garden
When through hot summers of WWII
Over the Lehigh River bridge
I carried our baskets of produce
Hoards for winter storage
Festive salads on our Italian table
Those medleys of color and chord.

That very eve of the big Spring change
The crescent first moon
Hung phosphorescent and alone
Except for Venus
Minding the ladle
As my friend Rik explained
Whose growth on his prostate
Is to be cut come Monday prime.

## Too Soon Gone

A normal person can be ten
Three times in a life's span
First there are the children
And Saturday morning soccer spills
Too soon gone, too fast.
One wishes to be ten again
Then predictably grandchildren arrive
With their goals to tend
And muddy leggings to boot
Just as their parents did—not gone at all,
But two in one, revived each Fall.

But the one who squeezes the heart
Was not the last but the first
Oh to be ten again in '45
Joy it was to be alive
To know the thrill
When the church bells began
And one can still remember
At what stone in the pavement
One's foot was raised
As held in a photographic still
Like planted in air
Never to surrender.
Then commenced soldiers' return
And pick-nicks like fairs
Block parties for three weeks
And backyards flowing with beer

Enough to bring closure
To our own wars of Thirty Years.
And the stories anticipated Technicolor
The mementoes, chevrons and lugers
Adding to the home-life treasure.
The kids trying to top each other

Who in conflict would be on their side
Ike or MacArthur
They stretched for the skies
Until finally one luck-minded child
Reaching high trumped all with God
The last choice and best ally
Upon which all forces could rely.

Not too long in the waiting
Came the great revivals.
Baseball, inadequate for the duration,
Regained its play as "majors"
Just as it was in '41
The last memorable season,
Its records still intact.
DiMaggio, Williams and Feller
Back to resume their positions
And New York with three teams packed
Each cheered by men wearing hats.
And boxing, the only other national action,
Received its reigning champ,
Joe Louis, who gave the black man pride,
Before Jackie opened the gates with his slide,
And we all gathered on the front door stoop
To hear epic battles,
Trilogies of sport, Graziano and Zale,
Robinson and LaMotta
When the middle weights were kings
And dominated the rings.

But such times could not linger
Come '52 and '3
I had other stories to learn
I was no longer ten
But pushing seventeen
Now cousins and friends
Were killed or captured
By the Chinese Yalu trap

And MacArthur's blind folly
Now soldiers came home
But by prisoners' exchange
Silent, uncheered by an unsteady nation
Too soon, too fast
The hastening winds of change.

We can never be young again
As we were at war's end.
But nothing can ever suspend,
No arguments however rife
Can ever dim the glisten
Of the moments we shared
When our eyes were only ten
And all things complied
With the glories of those men.

# Early and Late: The Hazards of the Ways

Tsi Giovan claimed it for the Italians
Big Mike rose to his full height
And insisted it was the Irish
Who laid the great railroad track
Pounding the table with accented fist.
Could one really dissent
From such embodied voice?
Like Chaucer's monk
They eliminated any workings of choice.
They were men of the middle passage
Connecting the old with the new country
Who labored the ways for others to travel;
They were the courageous, the uprooted,
Who also bent deep in the mines
To bring up the coal, that fired the steam
That sent the giant machines
Like black birds of thunder screeching loud
Crisscrossing America's fruitful plains
Joining us all in the new Age of Steel,
Railroads comprising the central appeal.

Of this we kids had no conception
But enjoyed its means nonetheless
During WWII we scoured the tracks
Hunting for scraps of iron
That brought ten cents a pound
But always on the look-out
For Straity the railroad dick
Who could come swooping down
Waving his pistol
Carousing some shots
That put us on the run,
All the while laughing and taunting
Leaving him back a sure half-mile.
The railroad tracks were our roadways
To get where we were going

Even hitching onto a slowing freight,
A wind-swept joy ride
Stretching with one hand outright
And one leg spread-eagle in flight.
And we not even ten
Well before the war's end.
We may have sensed but did not know
That death was all around us.
This world was our natural playground
With its own hard rules
Depression-bred, wartime-bound
The costly cut of human price.

Early and late
In the beginning and near its ending date
The railroads were chosen
As fitting emblems of our times
To convey our memories, our men—
A long-winding entourage of mourning—
From the great Lincoln
To the man who should have been.
It was the railroads that carried them
Through the lands of their natural constituency
Lincoln back to Springfield
And Bobby to the Arlington soil.
The people came together
Forming an unending honor guard
Unbroken strings along the iron rails
They pressed and massed tightly
Retinues of peopled swag
Pushing along the mounds of slag
Trying to keep pace
Or stay the trains in their carriage.

Thus children and grown men came together
As part of the same epochal reign
The young so happily unaware
But the old, they came to bear

The choices they were constrained to make
Their own fates obscurely present
Closing like manacles to where they were bound
They felt the tightened circles of iron
The circumscription of their ends.
Bobby saw them in the crowded mikes
Pointed like pistols to his head,
Their sacrifices were continuous, enduring
But without commensurate gain
Lincoln's work was done
But then undone by Jim Crow
Requiring another hundred years
Another tumultuous 'Sixties
That brought down Bobby
And continued the war
For five more years and 30,000 dead,
And the only President who resigned in disgrace
Thus decline like rot took hold
Auto makers with their freeways routed the trains
Simpler ways of coming together were derailed
And public service faltered and then failed
There was no way to cover the loss.
The auto created its own mischance
Breathing in its standing waste
Even increasing lanes brings no relief
By such means are we entangled
That all labor mars what it does.
There's no way out; we play a losing game,
Our own devices are countervailing gains.

But another lesson might here be derived
That men of greatness held in mind
When latching their belts
(With Dante, Shakespeare and Aeschylus)
That mortality attends each chosen way
That permanence and power cannot coincide
And that the means of our living
Is the trough of our demise.

## Shanksville

Whatever it was,
Needing a companion at 40,000 feet,
The accumulating spotty clouds
Suggesting the beetle bush wildness
That overhung his eyes;
The patches of ground below
That resembled the splotches
Of his over-ninety skin,
Or the flight path itself
Southeast of Pittsburgh,
Some twenty minutes from D.C.
Placing us directly over Shanksville,
The last great chapter of America's democracy,
All conspired to bring to mind
The presence that they required.
And so I said to the presiding form
The poetic father of us all
"Kitty Hawk, Kitty Hawk,"
And he, pleased by the recollection,
Replied, "Shanksville, a name quite different,
Like many along these rural roads,
But what's in a name?
What matters most are the revelations they contain."
Out of the depths of the American past,
He established the tableau of vision
That would govern our conversation.

The Wright brothers had it all,
The turn-of-the-century
Tinkerer's genius of invention
Coupled with the thirst for competition.
The French were dogging their tails.
But they were masters of locomotion
And at Kitty Hawk
Were the first to lift a powered device

Weighing more than air
Twenty feet off the ground for twenty seconds
A distance of 120 feet.
To the derision and abuse
Their claims elicited
Galileo's defense was ready for use:
"*Eppure si muove*," nevertheless it flew.
The French with justice in their hearts
Were brought round to admit and apologize
For discrediting this first adventure into space
That in more than a half-century's time
Would send a human to stroll on the moon.

With obvious delight
He foresaw the dimension of flight
But one event bewildered his sight
"We don't get much recent news
There where I am, so tell me about 9/11,
Some American character unfolded there."
Little did we realize, I began,
Those pigeons of flight
Would grow to be missiles of war.
Or that our planes would be turned against us.
We had an enemy who did not fear scorn
Who bound their young men to suicide missions
Shouting "Allah is great," while killing innocents.
And so we lost over 3000 by their blatant attacks.

With as much meaning as heroes can bear
Firemen of New York trudged the heavy stairs
Burdened with boots and bent with weighty wear
So dense was the jet-fuel smoke
That they paused at every few landings
To recover their shortened breath
And to calm and reassure the gathered folk,
Hurrying them down to safety
While they ignored such orders themselves.
Engine and ladder companies

Our soldiers, our knights
They mounted ever higher through the gloom
Marching unknowing to their doom.
When the buildings collapsed,
Bringing everything down
Filling the air with pulverized stone
And organic matter
My friend saw straight as was his habit:
"They did not fall, they are still climbing
But now it's Jacob's ladder
And God's soldiers are they."

I could not help but weep
As he uttered that prayer
For those brave men
Who were by selflessness inspired,
By their desire to help
To do more than the job required,
And brought to the plunging darkness a new light
That raised them to their original height.

On that carefree September day
The gods themselves must have turned away,
Why not a storm, even a trickle
Just enough to stagger delays
Put a stick in the spoke?
But they allowed this day
To run its habitual way
Maybe it was to lift ordinariness
To some unaccustomed sway.
The Wright brothers were skilled in locomotion
The FDNY were an elite corps
Who knew when they came running
That their country was at war;
But those on United 93
Were a mixed assortment of common folk
With no greater purpose in mind.
How did they rise up to blunt the design

Of the fourth plane smashing into D.C.
With a payload of nasty combustion
And obliterate Congress then in session?

The fuel-loaded non-stop to San Francisco
Began a wide-sweeping turn before Cleveland
A veer that brought them southeast of Pittsburgh
Only then did the captives overcome
Their last hope that restrains action.
While pestered by daily anxieties
There is in humans a reluctance to admit
The presence of the apocalypse
That they might be sitting in its midst;
No one imagines being injured in a taxi-cab;
At the first rumblings of Vesuvius
Pompeians should have run for their lives;
And in Krakow they should have reached for their knives.
But we will linger, we will stay
Until the knock on the door
Wakens the terror unacknowledged before.
Is it simply a fidelity to choice,
A failure to read the signals,
An ease of being in the quotidian rounds,
Which is normally shown to be right?
But it only takes one event, one mischance
Such comfortings to disperse
Facing us with horrors we could not rehearse
That we are where we are and not somewhere else.

So how did this assorted group
Figure the odds were against them,
Piecing together bits of information
And meeting together conclude
That after the WTC, the Pentagon
They too were on a mission that had one end,
A one-way flight to a bitter finale,
A red ball of fire
A dragon of wrath

Devouring every thing in its path?
They thought and accepted where their thought led.
Common people, some a bit more than ordinary,
Came together and made their choice,
One not of their choosing,
But chose the death that others might live.
There is no courage commensurate with this.
And so they charged together
A wild roar from Hell's gate
And fell only minutes, maybe seconds short
Of wrenching the plane from its downward course
That tore its way
Through the lush countryside
Of south western Pennsylvania
By rural route 219
Where everything was ordinary
The elements smelled so fresh and clean.

All perished knowingly
But their actions shall live
As models to unfold
Of the American character;
Circumstances will differ
But the basics remain
Calculation and bravery
Precision and moral courage
How can that abate?
Citizens of a republic,
Not subjects of a State.

Robert Frost mulled the account
Absorbed it to its full
Then smacked his thigh and stood up
Radiating pride at the way
His people responded
In the cabins of peace and war
They thought it through with mind and valor,
He departed at an opening in the cumulus

Still striding like Achilleus hearing Odysseus
Tell the exploits of his son Neoptolemus.

Dispute will always attend heroic actions
As the Wright brothers themselves can confirm,
Particularly in times when imaginative fervor
Lags and understanding has a distorted lens.
We cannot place in physical form
The living images that such actions adorn
Our people—the multitudes of the wise—
Benefitted from centuries of schooling
In the arts of life's hidden measures
And thus were able to provide
What the unrepeatable moment required
Heroic rightness of thought
A valor in act, those living virtues
That not even martyrdom denied.

# ABUSIVES (1-5)

## 1. Trucker

A burly roadster type
More bovine than bullish
Knew he caught her eye
Leaning over his bench's rest
He sallied an inviting smile
Stolid she faced, idling by the siding
He rose to collect his bags and stuff
Worked a path down the exit hall
She waited—not long after all—
With robot steps following his claim
Toward the men's John
Where he had readied a stall
His language was abusive
The hurt she wanted to share
She voiced her appeals
But took what she craved
Absorbent and without much care
Later under a hot shower
She washed herself clean
Thinking chance encounters
Cost less than they seem.

## 2. The Teacher's Sub

How sweet it can be
To shake memory's tree
And watch the leaves drift downward
To fill the sunken garnish bowl.
Special ones there to retrieve.

My favorite goes back to WWII
As a teacher sub in eastern Pennsylvania
And my husband way off in Australia
He sent cumquats home
Exotics for that region to savor.

I could detect the adoration
In Walter's eyes
So eager to help
To carry books and papers to my car
And then to my apartment door
And then strewn over the bedroom floor

His modesty was appealing
He feared he was too small
Or did not know where to begin
Or how to end
I reassured him on all these matters
Telling him to pay no mind
We were two parts of a swelling measure
Which he would know soon enough
An indeed he did
He shuddered and grabbed to take hold
Barely wetting his straining tip
And I, in my turmoil, bit him on the lip.

We visited again and again
He soon leading the way
He was called "teacher's pet"
By those Ignorant of its full extent

I passed all these things in mind
His little boy's peter
So slender sweet to the taste
The freshet smell my camel coat retained
Which I never had cleaned.

Oh those years of memory
How tender when they loosen
When I broke him as a colt—
And he rode me like a mare.

## 3. Tante Circe

In France it was the aunt
Whose duty was bid
To help the young pubescent
Learn his passageway
Lessons in the *ars amatoria*
Whose essence has always been
To control the self and ease the other.

When after a final rendez-vous
They joined the expectant family
All knew tutelage was complete
The dark arts of Circe
Had guided her pupil home
With a final kiss
She bestowed her diplôme,
*"je suis fière de toi."*
Fully aware that no ineptness
Would poison his well of life.

## 4. Marlene

"Orders were for sailing."
Against the iron rules of a material world
She sought to bring bounty and cheer
A pleasure at last equal to their imagining
They were her soldier knights
She loved to rub their fuzzy hair
So handsome brave and bright
So she bedded them
In town apartment or barrack bunk
What was there to spare
Against the odds of trench warfare?

Though she played at Lola and Concha
That was not where her true heart stayed
It was in pity for these young men
Sons of women
And by women restored
But not from the ravages of war
In the midst of pleasure she prayed
O Lord, bring them back steady and whole
So they might recall these times
When we opened ourselves
To each other
And somehow redeemed our crimes.

## 5. Birds of a Different Feather

He blinked his eyes at first glimmer of light
Puffed his feathery chest
Chirped some throat-clearing notes
And fanned out his archway colors
Particularly the blues so magnificently bright.

Today he would circle his favorite branch
A never failing catch
How could he falter
With such flags to unfurl
And colors to brandish
Fanning them in flight
Trolling what was his personal ranch.

Pickings proved sparse
Until one timid hen
All got up in coordinate grays
Emerged from the thicket of growth
Following the path by him laid out
An opportunity to spread his spray.

He began showing his stuff
But his loops in the air
Exposing his archway bright
Did not draw a peep from the graysome hen
Not even an oh, or ah
Like women responding to fireworks at night

She set herself down prim—
But squarely—in the middle of a limb
As if expecting her service of tea
Or her parasol from a leafy tree
He fluttered all the more
Trying to stir her staid demeanor
But that fostered no movement at all
Finally the climax of any show
He hung from the bough
With his archway feathers falling over his beak
Offering all the pleasures of life underneath

But this advanced art of plotting
Produced not even a parting nod
She bore no thoughts for his world
And her indifference made him sputter
The grey was simply wandering off
A moving target was no fun at all—
Like trying to top a rolling ball—
A lost prey that grey
So common in every detail
And him still hanging
His colors festooned to no avail.

## Sudden Glory

Against a time of ownership and sustainables
My father was committed to divestment
Like the deposed English kings
Mounting gestures of the self
And lo! they regain their sudden glory
How else explain
His bestowing 14 gold coins on Yenz
A purely somewhat friend?

He was from the century's uprooted
Bearing twisted tales
From a corner of Spain
Shadows from another being
Clamoring for the light
When lifted by his barroom buddies
He steps from chair to chair
A glass of beer balanced on his head
Not a twit of tilt
Not a drop spilt.

Or when his Casino betting partners
Come round to welcome "Pops" back
And cheer him on
Then he would order scotch and sodas for his gang
—an entourage fit for a president—
And would strut the bar as royal resident.

But please remember this:
In the dead of winter he fed the birds
With cupped hands tossing crumbs
Over the ice-bound earth
That parsed not a stubble of seed.
*O vous qui m'avez vêtu au temps de la froideur.*

Finally his rampant spirit can rest
His grave sited on a shelved plateau
With unending lengths of leveled stones
Laced, hemmed in and compacted
With his own ligaments of snow.

Unvisited perhaps, but not unperpetuated
It lived down from son to last son
Who strode the rooftop in splendid show
His blond hair streaming like banners in the wind
With hose in hand blasting the cluttered leaves
From out their tile sheaves
Sending them down the gutter spouts
To God knows where and whereabouts.

Such heights
So unlike life's daily monotone
Where all cluster, huddle
So hard to live down
When the deadly gene sets in,
Its victims long in hand.

## Oswego

I swung the baton like a baseball bat
Its rubberized cap sent careening off
Smack into the hall mirror shattered
Seven years bad luck, harped my maiden aunt
By another account many more than that.

I wandered down unknown places
Looking for a glazier on Oswego street
In an abandoned industrial plant
They never knew of such a thing;
So I tried "glass" instead
Eliciting what was like a scoff
Some such thing they in their past
But not very prevalent now—
Pointing to the walls' naked spaces
I then began to survey the place
Sunken walls and earthen floors
No ceilings to speak of or doors
Only heavy overhanging clouds
Whose rain ran color of rusted cans
Broken pipes clung vertically
Like ivy dripping gooey sounds
I really doubted this was my station
When from out a mound of refuse
Some kind of collective clothing bin
I caught letters of a mangled sign
"wego"

I offered to shake hands
But they had lost touch with that gesture
For which I was much relieved
Their arms were as floppy as gelatin
They might have been humanoid fish
So sub-primitive was their condition
They did not even scratch upon the walls

But walked about in small bands
Muttering sounds yet speaking through hands
As their circles began to close
With their toothless yaps and maws
I tried to flee but then broke stride
And to consciousness came rushing back.

In worlds to come
After centuries long past
Men will know that good things cannot last
And that even the best collapse
But there's no way they could tell
Of a downfall such as this
Of humans so utterly devoid
And of places unstoried even by hell.

## The Turn of the Stare

She hesitated in the hallway
And turned to stare
More meaningful than that
But less than a glare
Charged with hurt and confusion.
No squalor, fiasco, not even a bungle—
Too true to each for such missteps
Still there was pain and disappointment
Hanging in the air
From where he sat confounded
He wanted to burst and hold her tight
But neither moved.
In solitary stillness each held place
Was it just a woman not completing desire,
Or was he too bold in pursuit, too pointed,
Did she want him to wash her free,
Did she fault him—for what?
For not making her want him more
But that was a complex of female score
That wants her will swept away
But he lacked that calculating sway
That mechanism of contrivance
That passes for maturity
Of baubles and patter the sonorous array
A game neither he nor she were willing to play.

So friends they remained
Exchanging poems and learned essays
Letters sealed with warmth
But not forgetting the pause in the hallway
The fixed stare
That told of all that had been missing there.

PART TWO
# New Poems

## The Crow

Grounded but still brassy
Upstart while all but dazed
Snug fellow of the wanton fly ways
Far from your post
You tumbled into our roost
The hood's warmth taking for a bed
You stood better as a figurehead.

Oh buddy, young crow
You want nothing and give nothing in return
Except your unblinking stare
Corvus, croac, cah cah
Your statuary ware
Has long lost
The feathery gloss
Now like lacquered veneer
In falling shades of black
Like a Rothko painting
Or the panther I cast
In my third-grade art class.

There's much Americana to your wing
Pilgrims clad in uninviting black
Dust bowl survivors
Trying to find their ways back
Whose crease-lined faces
Are filled with sand
Claim you for their own
You are their god of forlorn
Their model in flight and makeshift
They have your staunchest stare
And all the sufficiency that was intended there.

You were perched on Ulysses' right shoulder
When he drew out through the narrows
Out onto the pathless sea
Fought the pull of Brasília's reaches
Just he himself and the circling skies
Such silent facing of the silent deep
Scared Dante halfway out of Hell.
You're not literature's favorite species.
The unmarked grave is your making.

Your brazen manner suits you right
Your singularity sets you free
Your ship burned and cables cut
The homing instinct is not your style
You feast on garbage dumps
And lighted parking lots
Anyways is how you thrive.

That's all the meaning you afford
Presence to your own accord
Meeting with that which is
You satisfy in the course of flight
You need no anchor to set you right
Embellishments fitting the prince of night
You are the thing itself
The only it it could want
Master of its own surmise.

## Coda for the Crow

The bold crow who stumbled into our garage was nurtured back to health in a few days. We placed him in our backyard where he could find seeds and other edibles. Very soon, he was joined by a gaggle of croaking crows and soon disappeared. We would never see him again. But two days later, rummaging through the yard, I came upon a crow's shorn wing. Thus, I concluded, even Huckleberry Finn went out West to be hanged.

But a poem is not undone by matters of fact
It does not require afterwards and aftermaths
Poems have their own fabled content
Their own schedules in time
Their own retinues of retention
Their happenings are fellows of kind
Surprises from the tunneling of mind.

Poems have their own stories to tell
Their own CV's, recognitions
All responding to their natural fit
A poem marks its own completion
Its own domain—
Where all good things connect.

A poem cannot be a total picture
Four corners of a flawless globe
It does not include all the cases
Even the exceptions that prove the rule
Mere intrusions, conversation's tool
It has what it wants
All its parts in full accord
What the crow meant
Wherever it still stands
Whether or not with wing shorn.

## 19 Men

In the thickening summer of fruit and fire
19 men stood athwart the flames
19 men trapped by the winds of change
Fronting the south winds was tough enough
Cutting and sawing to hack the breaks
Where the raging fire would consume itself.
Capriciously the wind changed its color
They knew they were in for trouble
Their spotter signaled the alarm
The fire had turned its teeth
They had to race toward a clearing
But with 50 pounds they were weighted
The dark smoke blinding view
No human unencumbered can outrun a fire
With a resinous stash of fuel
Chaparral, manzanita all primed
To give a jump to the flames
Bludgeoning legs of pounding fire
Reaching 40 miles per hour
Outmanned their only refuge, outgunned
Were the sheltering tents of aluminum
That could deflect the heat but not fend the flames
No widow's walks in this accounting.
Only their cell phones that lay panting.

It took their searchers hours
The bodies all together huddled
They needed bulldozers to lift the crew
19 white cars brought the bodies through town
As the entourage passed
Older women who knew these mother's sons
Snapped to a sharp salute
While rivulets overran their faces.

They were an elite crew
Home-grown boys
Well-trained and well-equipped
The Granite Mountain Hotshots
Come down from Prescott
To assist in Yarnell Valley
Subdivisions encroaching on the wilds
Propane tanks ready to explode
All the signs were there
High temperatures, drought, resinous fuel
But they were onto "the path of fire,"
Working to make some fireman's unit
Jocular laughing all the way
When a grim fortitude was needed that day.

We know their clear ambition
But what motivated them is a bit obscure
What roused them this summer season
Where foreboding ran along the rim
Of southwestern USA
Certainly it was the rush of victory
The pride of functioning well
Or was it something else
Doing battle with a more elemental power
They did not bother much about gods
What the ancients revered as power and presence
Air, water, earth and fire
Fickle, unpredictable, recurrent and jealously vain
Their powers contained not defeated
They simply subside when their business is done
They wait their turn to come again
To redress and reclaim their own,
The whelming ocean, the tangled brush
Properties they may have relinquished
But not forsworn
They play a stalking game
When the seasonal provisions are there
For the taking

Careful captains insist
Their men did not buckle or break
And point to how they were found
Braced together in a pyre-like mound
19 men burned in a unit
Fire, carbon monoxide and strangled air
And if they had run
What fault was there in that?
We have witnessed people leap
From 130 stories to escape the fire
The body seeks its own right to life
Quite different from machinery of mind
Suicides will leap from bridges
But halfway down the body
Will send its legs churning
To find some specimen of stable ground.
So there is no weakness, here, dispraise or blame

If the men broke to avoid the flame
They saw into the maw of death
Hell Gate's furnace of fiery mass
But their minds held together with friends of need
And managed to gather some part of reprieve.

Did they or didn't they does not much matter
Their mound of death is a holocaust
That transformed by imagination's core
Becomes the symbol of the 19 men
And our warrant shall be to picture them
Pitched together, we ask no more.

# Broken Lilacs

Broken lilacs along the strand
Broken lilacs come to hand
Moving slowly toward the West
No compass directing her steps
Daughter of woman
What was taken
Was freely given
No despondency there or regrets
She lived above the line of reproach
A trek her life needed to take
Part assignment, part choice
A woman's will was her own will
No thoughts detained her mind
Except an assurance in her glide
And the feel of her raiment
Caressingly entwined
Yet billowing free
At every lift of breeze.

The daughter of woman
By woman bestowed
Biological her stature
Yet separate her stare
Her mind was apart
Her reckoning real
Men were like puppy dogs
So needy in their appeal
She with ambling ease
Walked where she would
With a wave of hand and genial smile
Dismissed any fiercely growling mutt
"What are you so ferocious about?
Sent on its way, at heart appeased.

Though free from entanglements
Her own diaspora in store
Her embraces are true
Yet nothing can restrain
Where she lives by herself
A portion of living air
A segment of her will and way
She walks alone by the strand
Daughter of woman
Broken lilacs in hand.

# STATION CROSSINGS (1-9)

## 1. Harry

"The suicide kills the self and spares the other; the rational murderer kills the other and spares the self."
                                    - Albert Camus


**Harry, O Harry**
I would have wished the life longer
And even longer the rope
A wider expanse offered by hope
But foreclosed at 53
Homeless and jobless was no way to go.
So Harry took his leave.

Chivalrous and generous Harry
A mix-master deluxe
Always willing to tend the drinks
His hands at the full
At every gathering of friends
Expecting nothing in return
Except a nod to pataphysics,
Or was it isolation that he craved
Especially from crowds.
When in their midst
Waybegone and pinched.

Always present in health vigils
And peace marches
Ready to carry a sign.
But he left no signal
When he pitched himself off the gallows.
He spurned the hood
That might blinker his will
And launched into the void
Knowing that his well coiled noose
Would snap him back
His head would sag
And his legs would kick
With no place to land
And then dangle
With nothing to grasp by hand.

To your princely abandon
I offer this verse as prayer
Where you can rise and somewhat sustain
The determinations that you made
God's grace never came so close to home
As in that goodness by which Harry shone.

### i.
**She tanked the Cad**
Topping off for good measure
Parked it in the garage
With engine running
Wrote some mawkish notes
Like "It's been great"
Practically knocking the entire house out.

I wonder if in her last design
She gave thought
To those coming down the line
(I count three dead)
Who shared the fumes
That she left behind.

## 2. The End of Tragedy

"I have read all the books and the flesh is weary."

**Michelangelo imagined the scene**
Many times with his unerring eye
But never indifferently
Throughout he kept its three points
Its well-anchored triangular base
He could have completed it half-blind
Only with the resources of the mind
And yet his hand quavered
The conception was there
But not the terror of its returning stare
That told more than he wished to declare.

First at the top of the point
There is the young man all tangled
His horses no longer in hold
Jump their trees and pell-mell jangled
Drown out the music of the spheres
There all was blue, the sky, the water
On this sunny spring day.
The sort of day when things fall apart
As a message from the gods
Not to place much trust in human art

At the second plane a bevy of ladies
Lamentation and woe
To have seen what they have seen
 See what they see
Lifting their arms to scratch the eyes of heaven
How dare it be so calm when their prince is gone
Thrown from the vault of the secure serene
Their model of young manhood divine
He bounded the clouds like steps of a castle
They wanted his youth renewed as an eagle's

Not head over heels, arms flailing about
The routed confusion of his face
Howling all the way down
Into the diamond-surfaced deep
Like a meteorite fallen from its station

If you take our prince away
Who is there to compete
The slip-slopping boots of a barge man
In the darkness of the night?
Not our prince of morning
Coming with the force of light
Better to have died in war
Like so many others of his class
Make destitution complete

His chariot no longer a cabriolet
Where he stood like a young Apollo
A sun-god urging his steeds
Sleek and swift as whippets
Not orange crates banged together
Wrapped with crinkling crepe
His tousled hair...
His boyish hair by beauty bedecked
Leads back instead to dreams half-swept
Broken columns lining the shore
Nothing hangs together anymore
All torn from stations of right.

Woe woe is how they go
These sisters of grief unmatched
It only takes one to set them off
And then like cholera it spreads
Each outdoing the other in lament
This is the third point, the base line
While leaning in the lapping shore
A mature man, of the age of reason
Has witnessed this scene before

He wished they would not carry on so,
Acquire some casual human wit
All fall down, given the time
Even such knights in their prime.
Another young hero gone
What's one or more
Isn't that a shame?
Listen to these women complain
He turns to conceal his dry smile
That welcomes another to the shelf
While his flaccid penis floats
Wafted on the shifting tides.

But sadly even angels lend their assent
They laugh the loudest at tricks we turn.
Today we shine but tomorrow, tomorrow
Today's *affiches* we burn.

> **i. Wallet Poems IV.10**
> **He dropped the reins insolently by the shore**
> Picking his teeth with a haughty sneer.
> Through the riot of the pounding waves
> I appealed to any who might be near
> That I didn't even know the lout
> But who can make the sea understand
> She takes all things with equal hand.

## 3. Cruel Sufferer

I
Javert was not keen on forgiveness
Largesse was not his style
The way he learned was knuckles to the ground
So unlike Jean Valjean
Chosen foe to clog his days
The only foe he could not faze.
That man of easy charm
Whose affability stirs affection
People flock to his side
"Jean Valjean am I"
A name that resounds in its telling
In fact, doubling back on itself,
Like a retort from a canon shell.
Through his sundry levels of life
And many exchanges, it will emerge,
Bare its nicks and prison markings
Like lettered scars on a wounded tree
Love notes tossed in the rising sea
Or as a knight of chivalric honor
He cannot allow another
To bear the burdens that are his;
No one can stand in his stead
"Jean Valjean am I"
Not unmasked
But come forward at last.

The object become an obsession
Javert implacable, relentless
Who wears the law as his armor
And a hair-shirt under his vest
He never relents in his hunt
Why does he pursue so hard
The man whose arrest means his fall
The man whose capture will be his loss

The end of his purpose and of his cause,
The model that serves as goad to his chase
That part of himself he must erase?
His very being a living rebuke
The man he had wanted to be.
So even Javert puffs up on the name
His nostrils swell to discharge blame
"I arrest thee Jean Valjean,"
He loved to sing that song
It rang like justice itself

II
But the hunter becomes the hunted
And Javert with all his virtue
Is carried along
Even his solicitude
For the people's esteem
Does nothing earn him
But snickers smarting like lashes
They know the dimensions of his theme
That he is Jean Valjean's passenger
Like an insect on an eagle's wing
His victim has the touch of a king
Knows the palm lines of his life
Welcomes the fallen as returning brothers
Prodigals he takes into his home
Embraces sinners as atoned.
But Javert irreparable beyond recall
Begrudges every step
Cannot be brought to accept
That absence should receive the same pay
As those who plugged the toilsome day
Time is his menu of payment
That his ledger records in slices fine.
His cause is just, his reasons right
His heart, poor heart, knows no delight
What a shriveled and measured thing
Principle cannot take judgment's place

As card players of XXI announce
A scared game cannot win
Afraid of missing out he loses all
While Jean Valjean
With nothing to lose is free to fall.

**III**
Ah Javert, cruel sufferer
You paid the price
For your severe probity
And the articles of reproach
You taught in public squares
Exacting more than measures required
Your name shall rank in zealotry
Your body pinched by the medals you wear.

But more your mind
That cannot enter into social sprees
The cascades of silly noggins
The exchanges of nonsense
That betoken a larger communion
In the live scrabble of repartee.
Retreating down the pins of your life
To where it all started
The silences of the outcast
With a hornet's hive for mind
How did God allow this hybrid type—
Known only to human kind—
That wars with the better station
That race he yearned to join
The man he could have been
And so he mutinied against himself
Denied his regular regatta
And laid siege to his own estate
Like two ships grappling at sea
Neither can work itself free.
In pursuing Jean Valjean
He was cruel to others and pained in himself

To a double duty bound
Two persons in one are born
Strange doublings that fashion each other
Self-taught and self-creating partners in exchange
Crossings have not yet been conceived
Where such forces can room together.
One to suffer and the other to chastise.
Perversity unknown even to stations of the wise.

### i.
### And are there such differences
Between folk?
Don't they all swim in the same waters
Breathe in the same crossing smoke
Is it in their stations that difference matters?
Predestined to different ends
From brother to brother
Like Abel some walk with blessings full
While others strain rocks to push
And mud-stuck wagons to pull.

### ii.
### At length breaking a sullen silence
The honored guest
Pushed through to remark,
Grace is incremental,
To which Ralph replied,
In a gracious aside,
So is inhibition.

## 4. Charity and Carnality

**Charity and carnality are close to kin.**
Though they seem separated by sin.
Good doing gives pleasure to each
And pettifogging is *infra dig*
They never resort to the *sic!*
Careerism is not their model
They have no fear of failure
And its protective maneuver
They each take chances
Their faiths tell them
That after summer comes the Fall.
God's darkness covering all.

Dante was audacious enough
To place a courtesan in Paradise
Cunizza, sister to Ezzelino
One of the firebrands of Italy's North
From the same source
She traced the flame in her thighs
But rededicated herself to actions of the heart
The pleasures that did not smart
The favors of her past no longer trouble
As she understands the reasons for their being
The fuller goals that defined her meaning
Whence all her actions derived
And where they all were tending.

We can now see from the same root are they
Carnality and charity
The same fire moves them beyond any stay
So they forgive themselves the lot
And come together at the end
What literal-minded fail to comprehend.
Recognition of dissimilars.
Amounts to the reunion of pairs.

Each in-dwelling and outgoing.
Each would pick a penny from the ground
Or give shelter to a homeless man
Drunk flat-out in the street
Feed him, bathe his feet
Give him some money
Not asking what it's for
Even when he returns
And builds a lean-to
Down to alley scale
A cardboard domicile.
Where he will be receiving mail

A beating heart brings both together
Seeing beneath the encrusted nails
The hands that once held another
And traveled the waters with fuller sails.

>i.
>**All life dwindles**
>It singles down to this
>A woman lying with mouth open
>Abandoned to a precious kiss.

## 5. Her Books are in Order, Her Mind Intact

**Unusual as it was for a philosopher**
To employ a novelist's wares
It was Alfred North Whitehead
Who almost in an aside
Brought to our attention
How in the academy faculty wives
Are frequently the most alive.

He did not explain why this was so.
Perhaps it was their voices soft and low
("an excellent thing in woman")
No pneumatic thumping of legs,
Or hands clenched like claws
Bushels of names to enhance her cause
Or scratch from the list
Those the times have dismissed.

She was there for all to see
Not pinned to any bibliography
Yet did her critical reading bit
But favored Voltaire's *portatif*
What she could carry with her
She delighted to point out
That in Henry IV's address to sleep
Reference was simple and direct
Where all can recognize
The accumulated effect.

Allotted only Extension courses
She taught her students that memory was a curse
As she sat bundled in her camel hair coat
Contained, circumscribed
She was not a bumbler out of turn
Her speech was always on target
Not over-reaching or imprecise

Impeccable its flow
Delightfully given, delighted its tow.

She joined no learned society
But thought the Swifteans had merit
Stroking her husband's sleeves
She declared no substitute for knowledge
But added knowing itself was not enough
And most disputes ridiculous

A battle of the books
A jangling like cans attached
To a just married car
Their possessions are rental
Their holdings are partial
Their leases incomplete
What they return unused
Enjoins its own price
Life slipped through their fingers
Like cubes of melting ice.

Her moments alone
Came a few miles from home
When she stood on a cliff
Overlooking vast waters
And she could not conceive
How her crossing intentions
Could reach any station
Where only some few have swum.

Subdued but not submissive
She yielded to that lot
Toward which she was bent
And thought for her life
The mind entrusted to her
She returned its parts well spent.

**i.**
**Not once, not ever**
Did it happen,
In the world over,
As it did in America in '72
That one sister could claim to another.
"I am more intelligent than you."

## 6. This is my mother
##    (of whom I am very proud)

**Crossings describe the ways we go**
Stations explain why it is so.
Stations' larger order of perception
Takes things out of regular sense
Where they follow in a sequence
Keeping in track front and behind
But have no contact above and beyond
The one promises worldly ease
A coming into one's estate
The other brings a wrack of being
Alteration to a different state.
The one issues the soul at rest
The other calls it to a commanding test.
There is no choice in either of these ways
But to embrace one to the fullness of its days.

Crossings have mixed encounters with stations,
Said Anne to Mary,
—Words of a lifetime come together
Without summaries, without text—
Some are modest in their estimations
Some crossings are heavy with sanctions
Reckonings of a life that require their price
Tragedies not averted
Just waiting to answer their callings
Like name cards at a dinner table.

Your son was called out of his traces.
How much better it would have been
If the Sanhedrin had said, "Here's a local boy
Who attracts crowds by spinning parables
Let's cultivate his literary gifts
Take him under our wing,
Let's put him to work, work for goodness sake."

How much better for them, for us
It all would have been, for Jesus
Who was compelled to jump his crossing
Yield to his station, with nothing on his back
He left nothing behind, not even a shroud
Which absence became the stuff of legend
He separated from the ordinary world
Prayed that this cup might pass
And in his wounding became more holy
Some would even say divine.

The sorrowing mother Mary—
Rarely is a mother so intimate to story,
So elevated—is the daughter to her son
Who brings her forth from the shadows
Once her son was called past crossing
Inevitably she was enfolded too
When Jesus asked the cup to pass
She knew it was not for himself—no lapse—
But rather for her, to spare the double task
Imagining her son hardly conscious
Still writhing on the tree
She knew that from the moment he was born
From his first moment in life
Her motherly sense foresaw
The end he would endure
She wished it would stop
She doesn't desire God's eye
Whom did such a gift ever help?
Look what it did for Noah.
And the trouble that Ham partook.
Who saw his father naked
Hers the greater passion foretold,
To see her son twice dead
And her motherly chore
Then, as before, to take his body
Cleanse the wounds the world had made
The very wounds that grew so great

People found life in the damaged king
To their own lives so corresponding.
That young man of uncommon grace
The fallen god of mankind's embrace
Oh why was she, while still in crossing
Given the powers to foresee his end
And do nothing to prevent his torment
Powerless to resist their fates.

In his larger movements
The station to which he returned—
He formed part of a trinity
But even such a composite three
Had need of another
A mediator between two worlds
Mary, mediatrix and mother,
Her vision was her fate
 She could relate but not discharge
She remained in the crossing world
Washing the body she was forced to exhume
She took on a mother's function
She lifted the winding sheet
More than curious to see his manhood bare
Not like Ham, but with a mother's knowing,
Biological and spare
What is it that the Mother of God
Wished to observe buried in its bed of rest
A person of mass and spirit
The world over
She saw present and future
The onus of his bridge
The orchid of his plume
The vessel of his doom.
Forgiveness was her pledge.

There are those, Anne resumed,
Whose fortunes are their fate
For us our crossing is grief

For him the cross was his station
His calling out of life
But we shall cross over imperceptibly.
With not even a knot in time
We are the bearing ones
Who live between the lines.

    **i.**

**She trod with silver slippers**
Her golden hair gleaming
Through the doorway dark as night
Before enveloped by the closing waters
She uttered a shy farewell
To those whose future lay waiting
"Weep not for me;
Take heed for yourself and your children."
Though completely submerged
Her Sibylline voice trembled
Over the waters, while an aureole light
Lingered outlining her moving shade.
Sending ruffles of ripples to the other side
She rose to offer her arm to an escort
Come to instruct her in death's conclave.

## 7. Profusions of Song

I
Four Liverpudlians landed on these shores
Come to replenish our musical stores
From which they had taken so much—
Harmonics from the Everly Brothers
From Buddy the easy appeal,
And from Elvis the *force majeure*
But not the swivel hips; hardly Dionysian
Their musical demeanor was chaste
Unlike the dithyrambics of their followers
All wallowing in rapturous embrace
Ready to kiss the chocolate from their lips
Enough to persuade that talented scout
 Ed Sullivan to sign them on the spot
To two stints on the stage at CBS
And millions on national TV.
Their history had come into sight.

The four had been greater
Than the sum of their parts
But when intruders began to peel off
Their individual accounts
Their magic circle became a rubble
The solo undertakings less than their matter
Death followed upon disorder
Traveling through the dark woods
Where Dante says we all must wander
Death hung from the tangled boughs
Of serpentine trees
Glint snake-eyes fired unerringly
Its deadly fangs into guileless flesh
That's all it took those merciless days—
Call them what they were, Days of Assassins—
To turn the four into a remnant twain.

Who now, after a cycle of 50 years,
Are turned again to the CBS stage
Where they first came of age
Standing together as always winsome
Four again by spirit banded
Singing to overflowing gladness
Lifted the roof to heaven's ceiling
And the audience, there, or at home, or abroad
Joined them in song as if by chart
When it truly was by heart
Faces awash with cleansing tears
A golden treasury of delight
A magic circle formed so tight
It fended off death and dispersal
Making up its lacking length of years.
By the memories of intensity's height

**II**
Another cycle of 50 years
Retrieved that dread occasion dear
Of a riderless horse
And the heavy caisson's wagon wheels
Keeping time to the solemnity
That Chopin's Second yields
American testimonial: Spartan, austere.

Five-deep the people lined the august streets
An honor guard teeming, observant, protective
Guiding the young president to his rest
Too late as the glinted snake-eyes
Peering down a scope
Took its unimpeded way
And stopped the promise of a better day
Like Hamlet, he did not live to prove his mettle
Without redress, without recall
The bitterest cut of all.

And once again we relive the scene

Not Dallas, or D.C. but Chicago.
The center of American political life
When following the murder of its president
And three more assassinations
The Democrats split apart
And turmoil spilled onto the streets
And through the convention hall,
Where the spirit of mighty song
Rose up again and led a parade
Through the crowded stalls
Hailing the glory that marches on
And not to be ordered down
On and on they marched
To their promised land's proud tune
And as they marched their numbers grew
For 46 minutes they breathed the spirit
That brought them hither
Forming another magic circle
It's like not having been seen before
And when they stopped they did not falter
Not for want of breath or zeal
Having touched the height of appeal
They simply subsided
And when the time went dragging on
They held to what their truth attained:
All knew it could have been better.

Mayor Daley deserved better
He chose power over money
(And those ward heelers who chose wealth
Ended up losing both.)
And built Chicago into a modern city,
As Haussmann did to Paris
Or Sixtus V to Rome
Chicago was his city, his baby
And outside were rowdies
Intent on violating his child
His blind wrath prevented him from seeing

That they were his children as well.

Aeschylus, that soldier-poet
Would have understood
The entanglements of power
In whose winding ways America lives
To confirm his decree
That against our will we attain wisdom
The only country that beckons to tragedy.

## 8. Letters to the Home Place

He was their kid
Their image to see
Dressed in their colors
But then he jumped to another team
—Even the Mexican League would have been better—
Far over the waters
Dropped the flag, the banners
All the symbols of placement
On their genealogical tree.

They were prime, manly men
Who after the war
Worked with steel
Heavy duty lifting
Before the mills decamped
Following the wages
First to the South
Then overseas in stages
In despite of this Rust-belt recession
No crime occurred on their streets
Nor was it transported elsewhere.

They showered quickly
Before resuming their posts
A street corner society
Not mean spirited
Given to teasing at the most
Arms crossed with muscles blaring
With only wife-beater shirts for wear.

They would hang out
Until it was home for mother's dinner
But not before he appeared
With the day's scorecard
All delivered from his head

Who pitched, who scored, who hit
He was their chosen kid
College bound, a "natural"
Carrying their hopes and dreams
To places they had never been.

But by him the order was broken
He was called to another station
A calling that he heard and answered
A summons from beyond the grave
Saying all must be put at risk
He was one of Nietzsche's pioneers.
Bodily tattered and torn
On the barricades' barbs
Eternally divided
On his station's cross.

The home place still remains
Like ghosts from the past
Daily letters were his charge
Letters bearing no postage
To those men who are no more
But he will still write
As if wishing them to understand
That if he did abandon
Their colors, issues, their side
In following his choice
He was telling their time.

The cost of the action was the charge of the call
But expiation is the longest charge of all.
A mortgage never to be paid down
He will repatriate them as they stood there
Like horses milling in a corral.
No need to run, no place to go
The needle set on idle
As far as the mind can see
Waiting for the ball scores

And all they had to be shouting about
Waiting until eventide
Working men with a working man's pride.

Bring me back, he prays
Task me again
I'll do better, I promise
I'll offer a different show
But this pledge to the dead
Blows like dust off the grave.
There's not much to offer
Not much to save.

## 9. "The wisdom of the wise ..."

I
Interminable nexus of bonded things
The expatriate is always repatriated
As in mind he carries with him
House by house, door by door
The places and the names
That brought him about
He can never abandon or dislodge
They comprise the matter of his being
The chatter of his mind
How to separate bullion from the stew
Or sauces made into one ragout?
In their beings compounded
Are stations and crossings
Come together at the last.
As things bound fast.

What the Magi bring
What each they have been seeking
Is to be satisfied
They are the emblems of our class.
Recognition of a star
Commences a journey
Of powers with their own weights
But one needs a start
An impulse of direction
That begins with a crossing
And leads to a station
Complications of journeying
The hazards of the ways
The impediments of costly delays
And the circumventions of deceit
All these extended their journey
They travelled by night,
Better to avoid the heat, they explained

But better to follow the star
That was their guiding light
They required water and rest
Did not even worry over treasures
Heaving down their camels' sides
Eased their beasts to a sitting berth
In talk began to rehearse their days
They had come so far.
And might as well set down here
There before Mary
With the infant at her breast.
The star that they followed led to mother and child
In recognizance they bent their heads
And offered their gifts
Simple responses for simplicity's sake.

Was this the place to which they were brought?
And these the meanings they had always sought?
And if they chose to make it so
Upon whom could the joke be had?
Stargazers ending in a thatched stable
They looked at each other amazed
And broke a smile
Not even cushions around a table.
But having followed their own surmise
They now will know their own way back.
Which has always been the hardest track.

The circle of their journey is now complete
That which they seek.
Is in common hold
But each casts an image
That beguiles and is true
Each moment is weighted with signs
To which attention must be given
They all come together
Gestures and acts forming a figure in time.
Their minds lent in trust

To be returned in good order
Knowing to what ends
Their blessings were meant

## II
Portraits do not end at their frame
But stretching reach out
Extending their kind and name
To another genre, another claim
So stations and crossings
In the darkest nexus of the imaginary divide
After much trying of discourse
Why should they not collide
Resume their original content
Each defining the other
As they were at the beginning
Like pieces of a puzzle.
Each has a text to read, a part to fit
It is what it is but not by itself
With preludes and postludes
Still retaining a dominant setting
Such mingled powers bring exchange
Are enactments of a double purchase
Gifts of precious metals brought to all.

We are placer miners, panning a twisted lead
Up the sources where waters crest the stone
We read signs that are the markers
We have sown
Bent in their particular ways,
Impressions that have stuck
Become one with our days
There they were waiting
Forebodings wrapped in promise
That become as final as our forbears
There is a permanence in what passes
An order in the blessings that accrue
And in the disfigurements that scar

They are of our own choosing
Like portraits hung on mounting stairs
We have placed the figures there
The higher we go the deeper the stare
Pressing down with an imprinted force
The closer we get to the length of our years.

# LAGGARD

**Sue Hertel, the premier painter of our group,**
Dick Barnes, called by one who should know,
"The best poet in America,"
Add to them Denis O'Connor and Karl,
And you have a nifty Claremont troupe
The ornaments of a university town
Holding to all that art held true
Only the lineage of poets unnumbered.
How is it that they all are gone
And I am left still standing here?
But have no fear
Laggard soul that I am
I've grown accustomed to bringing up the rear

Ricardo Quinones is a scholar-critic, professor emeritus of Claremont McKenna College. He is the author of such prize-winning volumes as *The Changes of Cain: Violence and the Lost Brother in Cain-Abel Literature* (1991) and *Dualisms: The Agons of the Modern World* (2007), which was followed by *Erasmus and Voltaire: Why They Still Matter* (2010) and *North/South: The Great European Divide* (2016).

www.ingramcontent.com/pod-product-compliance
Lightning Source LLC
Chambersburg PA
CBHW032048290426
44110CB00012B/999